M000278320

ORDINATION
QUESTIONS

THE ORDINATION QUESTIONS

A Study for Church Officers

by
HOWARD L. RICE
and
CALVIN CHINN

Geneva Press
Louisville, Kentucky

PRINTED IN THE UNITED STATES OF AMERICA

13 14 15 16

Order from
Geneva Press
(800) 227-2872

ISBN-13: 978-0-664-50213-3
ISBN-10: 0-664-50213-X

CONTENTS

USING THIS STUDY BOOK

The purpose of this booklet is to help newly elected elders and deacons of the Presbyterian Church (U.S.A.) prepare for the offices and responsibilities to which they have been elected. The Form of Government is explicit about the need for preparation on the part of those who have been elected to church office. *"The minutes of session shall record the completion of a period of study and preparation, after which the session shall examine them as to their personal faith; knowledge of the doctrine, government, and discipline contained in the Constitution of the church; and the duties of the office"* (BO G-14.0205, italics added). The questions required for ordination are a summary of these required areas: faith, church doctrine, government, and discipline. As we answer the questions, we show our understanding of what the church requires and needs from its leaders.

This study is divided into eight sessions, covering the nine ordination questions. Each session includes a commentary on the question(s) and suggestions for reflection and action. Each participant should have a copy of this book, the *Book of Order,* the *Book of Confessions,* and the Bible. This book will be the

main study resource. Assignments in the other resources will be made from time to time.

It is intended that church officers engage in this
study together as a group. While it is possible for individuals to read and study this book on their own,
the suggestions for reflection and action encourage
group activities and discussions. They are intended
to assist participants to gain a clearer and deeper
understanding of the commentary on each question.
There may be more suggestions than can be used in
a single session. No time has been specified for each
session, in order to allow groups to adapt the study
to their particular settings and time limits. The ad-
ditional readings suggested at the end of each session
will assist participants in discussing the substance of
the session.

Abbreviations

BO—*The Book of Order, 1992–1993,* the Presbyter-
   ian Church (U.S.A.)
BC—*The Book of Confessions* (1991 edition), pub-
   lished by the Office of the General Assembly of
   the Presbyterian Church (U.S.A.)
G—Form of Government
D—Rules of Discipline
W—Directory for Worship

THE ORDINATION/
INSTALLATION QUESTIONS

One of the characteristics of the Presbyterian Church shared with other denominations in the Reformed family of churches is the practice of ordaining persons to the threefold ministry of minister of the Word and Sacrament, elder, and deacon. Other denominations may have officers with similar titles, but we of the Reformed tradition are unique in that we ordain people to church office who, in other denominations, are called lay people. The usual distinction between clergy and laity does not apply to us. *All* church members share in the ministry of the church. All people who join the church are required to profess their faith in Jesus Christ as Lord and Savior and to promise their willingness to participate in the life and mission of the church.

Church officers are called to particular responsibilities and authority within the body of the church. In order to ensure that they are committed to the work to which they are called, the church requires that they make very explicit affirmations that go beyond the essentials required of members. While membership vows are merely suggested in the Form of Government, the ordination/installation questions are specific, and the particular wording is required by the Constitution.

What is more, the ordination of elders and deacons is essentially the same as that for ministers of the Word and Sacrament. Persons are elected to serve in all three offices, they receive instruction in preparation for office, they answer the same Constitutional questions, and they are set apart by a governing body through the laying on of hands.

The Constitutional questions are for the purpose of making clear that those who bear responsibility within the church are willing to exercise that responsibility within the framework of the Constitution of the church. They must have a clear understanding of the purpose of the church, be sympathetic to its doctrine and government, and be prepared to accept the work that is before them. The ordination/installation questions are one way we have as a church of making sure that our officers will exercise authority within defined boundaries, which are the same for all officers.

A person is ordained as an elder, deacon, or minister of the Word and Sacrament in the Presbyterian Church (U.S.A.), and not just as an officer of a particular congregation. When, for example, an elder or deacon transfers membership from one particular church to another, a record of ordination accompanies the letter of transfer. The person will not be reordained in the second congregation if elected to the session or board of deacons.

Because all three ordained offices of our church share in leadership, the same questions are asked of those elected to the three offices. Only the last of the questions is different, for it pertains to the particular duties of the office. The only distinction among the different offices is their function.

The same questions are repeated each time a person is installed in office. At one time, ordination and election to church office meant that service was for life. Such life service made literal the meaning of the word "elder." The typical session was made up of people of quite advanced years. Only death, transfer of membership, or removal for heresy or misconduct could produce change in the composition of the session or board of deacons. The present mandatory rotation system in the Constitution of the church requires that elders and deacons may not serve more than six consecutive years before they must be replaced (BO G-14.0200). Rotation permits flexibility and the inclusion of many more people in the leadership of each congregation. It also places emphasis upon ordination to a particular function rather than

to a special class of people. The function of installation is not unlike reordination to function. Even
though ordination is for life, a pastor, elder, or deacon is installed each time that person is elected to
particular active service.

The Constitution of our church is not a static doc-
ument. It can be amended by action of the General
Assembly and approval by the presbyteries. The or-
dination/installation questions can thus be changed.
These changes are one reason why it is important to
ask the questions each time a person is installed in
office. At the time of ordination, a person may have
answered questions that were different from the
questions that are now required.

Some people are disturbed by changes in the or-
dination/installation questions. We must recognize,
however, that changes in wording are an acknowledgment of different understandings by the church
that take place over the years. The Constitution now
requires, for example, that both men and women be
elected to the offices of elder and deacon, as well as
to the ministry of the Word and Sacrament (G-
6.0105; 14.0201). Those persons who cannot accept
the ordination of women are unable to accept leadership in the church. It would make no sense to ordain
people as leaders who are not in harmony with basic
principles by which the church understands itself.

During this course of study, we will examine each of the required questions in order to understand what is expected of us as ordained officers in the Presbyterian Church.

Suggestions for Reflection and Action

1. In groups of four, discuss the following questions: How do you feel about the fact that, in the Presbyterian Church, ministers, elders, and deacons share a common ordination and that the usual distinction between clergy and laity does not apply? How does this change your view of the office to which you have been called?

When ready, return to the larger group and share your responses.

2. Individually, jot down some of the reasons why the wording is so specific and particular for the ordination/installation questions.

When the large group convenes, share your reasons.

3. How does the Presbyterian Form of Government determine our understanding of ordination beyond the local church?

Discuss in triads (threes), and then share with the larger group.

4. What are some advantages and some disadvantages of limited terms of service?

Discuss in one large group.

5. Why is it necessary to ask the ordination questions each time a person is installed in office? Discuss in one large group.

Additional Reading

BO G-6.0100, 6.0200, 6.0300, 6.0400
BO G-14.0200
BO G-3.0000
BO W-6.0000—W-7.7000
Acts 14:23
1 Timothy 5:17–22

THE CHURCH
AND ITS LORD

QUESTION ONE: "Do you trust in Jesus Christ your Savior, acknowledge him Lord of all and Head of the church, and through him believe in one God, Father, Son, and Holy Spirit?" (BO G-14.0207a)

Profession of faith in Jesus Christ is so central to the identity of all Christians that it cannot be taken for granted. Those who are set apart by ordination are thus required to reaffirm their commitment to Christ. He is the one who was born truly human, sharing our life fully. He is also the one we confess to be the true and complete revelation of God. In Christ we discover the meaning and purpose of all that God intends for human life.

As we answer this first question we confess that Jesus Christ is trustworthy. We know in our own experience that he is the one who provides us with the grace to accept ourselves by making it possible for us to believe that we are forgiven by God and set

15

free from the power of sin and evil. All other objects of human trust are sooner or later doomed to disappoint us. When we trust ourselves, we despair over our lack of clear purpose, our compromises with evil, our false pretenses. When we trust other people, they reveal that they are not what they seem to be either. They show us the very weaknesses which we know only too well in ourselves. We trust human institutions only to discover that they use us for their own purposes. Jesus Christ is trustworthy because he unites word and deed in harmony, saying and doing truth in all situations.

We trust Christ as our Savior. He saves us from ourselves, from the consequences of our selfishness, pride, and hopelessness about life. He saves us from our tendency to self-destruction and emptiness in the face of death. He sets us free so that we can love and forgive other people. In his death and resurrection, we believe, God opened for us the way to new and eternal life.

We acknowledge him as Lord of all. No part of life is beyond his redeeming reach. He is Lord of our personal life, guiding us in difficult decisions, assisting us when we are discouraged, and providing hope and strength in our weakness. He is Lord of interpersonal life, enabling us to forgive as we are forgiven. He shows us the meaning of absolute acceptance of others. We cannot condemn others when we see them from Christ's perspective. He is Lord of the structures of family, work, and the social order. His witness condemns all human efforts to deny some people the fullness of life while providing special privilege for others. He is the judge of human wrongdoing and the evil in human structures, and is the hope of the suffering and downtrodden. He stands alongside the helpless as one of them and one with them.

As officers of the church of Jesus Christ, we acknowledge that we are not ultimately in charge. The church does not belong to us. We are called to exercise leadership by the One who provides both judgment and example. When we make decisions in the church, we must reflect his will and not merely our own opinions. To acknowledge Christ as Lord of the church is to be accountable to him for our actions and to seek his guidance.

Christ is the head of the church of which we are members. No analogy is more powerful than that of the church as the body of Christ. Each of us is part of the whole. As do the parts of a human body, we function best when we do that for which each of us is best equipped by talent and experience. Our individual uniqueness is part of our calling. We must not pretend that we are alike. We declare that as a

human body has a head and the head is the source
of direction for the rest of the body, so Christ is the
one who provides direction for what we do.

As the revelation of God, Christ provides our primary image of God, that of the Trinity. This central
mystery of our faith is always beyond our full understanding. We affirm that Christ provides us with
all we need to understand about God. This is the God
who created all that is, called Israel to be a special
covenant people, redeemed it from slavery in Egypt,
gave it the Land of Promise, and, when Israel forgot,
sent prophets to declare truth and remind the people
of God's intention. Following centuries of tradition,
the ordination question calls this creating, covenant-
ing, redeeming God "Father." In spite of the dangers
of making God into a masculine idol, it is very difficult to replace the term "Father" with another.

Declaring God as Son is the recognition of God's redeeming act in providing the long-awaited Messiah
of Israel to be the Savior of the whole world. God as
Son is God incarnate with us. Although one with us
in our humanity, Jesus is uniquely God with us.

The Holy Spirit is God's continuing presence
among us, working wherever two or three are gath-
ered together, making it possible for us to live in love
and harmony with one another. The Holy Spirit
opens our minds to perceive the Word of God in Holy
Scripture and enables us to dare to accept that Word.

As we affirm this ordination/installation question, we make a primary commitment to Jesus Christ. All other commitments are secondary and flow from this one.

Suggestions for Reflection and Action

1. Individually, recall the occasion when you made your public profession of faith in Jesus Christ as your Lord and Savior. Jot down on a piece of paper everything you can remember about the occasion— such as place, year, people, age, feelings.

Next, compare that experience with your present experience of reaffirming that commitment. Write down the similarities and differences.

2. Write your name on a three- by five-inch card.

Write three words that would communicate to a total stranger that your faith in Jesus Christ is central to your identity.

Pin your name tag on your clothing, and mix with other class members, reading one another's responses.

3. Reread the second and third paragraphs, which deal with the trustworthiness of Christ. Now use the following reader reaction method: Put (!) at those points that stimulate a new idea or bring a new insight; (X) at those points at which you disagree with the writer; and (?) at those points that are unclear or which you would like to discuss.

Compare your responses with the rest of the group in open discussion.

4. A longtime, active member of the church writes an angry letter to the session, threatening to leave the church over the session's action to affirm and support nuclear disarmament. The irate member argues that the church should have nothing to do with politics and other "secular" matters.

How would you respond to this irate church member? How does your affirmative response to this first ordination question inform your response?

Share your response with responses of others in triads, and then with the whole group.

5. Reread the paragraphs on the Trinity. How does the absence of any part of the Trinity leave us with an incomplete image of God?

Discuss in triads, and then share with the whole group.

Additional Reading

BO G-1.0100
BO G-1.0307
Westminster Confession of Faith, Ch. VIII,
BC 6.043–6.050
Confession of 1967, Part I, Section A.1,
BC 9.08–9.14
Brief Statement of Faith, BC 10.2
1 Corinthians 12:12–26
Colossians 1:15–20
Ephesians 4:11–16

THE AUTHORITY
OF SCRIPTURE

QUESTION TWO: "Do you accept the Scriptures of the Old and New Testaments to be, by the Holy Spirit, the unique and authoritative witness to Jesus Christ in the Church universal, and God's Word to you?" (BO G-14.0207b)

This question is both second in order and second in importance. Scripture is subordinate to Jesus Christ, who is the living Word of God. We understand all Scriptures through Jesus Christ, who illumines that which is otherwise obscure. His radical love and acceptance of all people is the measure by which we read all other parts of Scripture.

In order to be faithful to its Lord, the church must examine its life by Scripture, which is both unique and authoritative. All other regulations, confessions, and procedures are subordinate to Scripture (G-2.0200). Scripture tests our actions to determine if our witness is faithful, our love broad enough, and our corporate life inclusive enough.

The whole Bible functions authoritatively in the life of the church. The Old and New Testaments are equally important for us under the authority of Christ. The Old Testament is not less inspired than the New, nor is it less a witness to Jesus Christ. Without the Old Testament, the New Testament cannot be understood and the demand of God for justice can be privatized or comprised. Without the New Testament, the Old Testament can be reduced to a set of laws to be obeyed. Thus the ordination/ installation question requires us to acknowledge that both Testaments are unique and authoritative.

We who lead the people of God do not make decisions solely on the basis of what we think is best or most practical. If we do this, we make ourselves the final authority. Without clear obedience to higher authority, we are in danger of losing touch with who we are and what we are called to be and do. Scripture holds us accountable to the One who calls us into the church and sends us out into the world as disciples.

Continuity with the record of Scripture keeps us honest and prevents us from idolatry of ourselves, from captivity to persons with great power who might persuade us or to the powers of this world that seek to control the church and use it for their own ends.

The authority of Scripture demands a response. We live out the meaning of that authority when we struggle together to be faithful to God's guidance. The authors of the Barmen Declaration, speaking to the German Evangelical Church, dared to say, "If you find that we are speaking contrary to Scripture, then do not listen to us! But if you find that we are taking our stand upon Scripture, then let no fear or temptation keep you from treading with us the path of faith and obedience to the Word of God . . . " (BC 8.04, The Theological Declaration of Barmen, Ch. I).

This is no easy task. Much evil is done in the name of the Bible. A verse can be taken out of context and used to justify any idea. Christians have sought to justify slavery, the subordination of women, warfare, and financial greed on the basis of particular isolated passages. The Westminster Confession of Faith acknowledges the difficulty of interpreting Scripture: "All things in Scripture are not alike plain in themselves, nor alike clear unto all . . . " (BC 6.007).

Ordained ministers of the Word and Sacrament have special education, including the study of Greek and Hebrew, which prepares them to assist the rest of us in the interpretation of Scripture. Yet we are all responsible to be faithful students of the Bible. Among the duties of elders listed in the Form of Government is the following: "They should cultivate their ability to teach the Bible and may be authorized to supply places which are without the regular ministry of the Word and Sacrament" (BO G-6.0304).

The Westminster Confession of Faith provides challenge and encouragement for us all: " . . . those things which are necessary to be known, believed, and observed, for salvation, are so clearly propounded and opened in some place of Scripture or other, that not only the learned, but the unlearned, in a due use of the ordinary means, may attain unto a sufficient understanding of them" (BC 6.007). These ordinary means of understanding Scripture include: a willingness to listen to others who may understand the Bible differently; a proper hesitation about too rapidly drawing our own conclusions about the meaning, being willing to devote serious time to study of Scripture in the context of the whole; and a humble submission to the work of the Holy Spirit.

The authority of the Bible is "the Holy Spirit." As we read the Bible prayerfully, patiently, and corporately, we dare to trust that the Holy Spirit will open our minds to comprehend and obey God's will. Because the meaning of Scripture is not always self-evident, our willingness to be led by the Spirit is submission to the ongoing inspiration that enlivens the written words for us today.

The concluding phrase of the ordination question is the most personal and direct. The Scriptures are to be accepted as "God's Word to you." We are to lead the people as we are nourished and sustained by God's revelation. As we, ourselves, read the Bible prayerfully and regularly, our own lives are addressed, our temptations are described, our failures are pointed out, and our forgiveness is promised.

Suggestions for Reflection and Action

1. Learning that a divorced person is seeking membership in the church, three families have written to urge the session to refuse church membership to this person on scriptural grounds.

How would you respond to these families? How does your affirmative response to this second ordination question guide and inform your response?

Share your response in triads and then with the whole group.

2. The session has been asked by the congregation to address the question: Who owns the church property?

Rank from highest (1) to lowest (4) where you would actually go for guidance:

_____ the *Book of Order*   _____ a lawyer

_____ the Bible   _____ the church bylaws

Discuss your priority ranking with one other person. Then share with the whole group.

3. Write down on a piece of paper your three favorite texts from the New Testament.

Now write down your three favorite texts from the Old Testament.

Working individually, reflect on these questions: Was one of these lists harder to do? Do you limit your Bible-reading?

4. The pastor has been hospitalized suddenly and will be absent from the pulpit for at least a month. After much discussion, the session has decided to take seriously its responsibility to "supply places which are without the regular ministry of the Word and Sacrament" (G-6.0304). You are one of the elders who has volunteered to fill the pulpit for one of the Sundays. What steps will you take to prepare yourself to preach in two weeks?

In the normal life and work of the church, how would you exercise this responsibility to develop and use necessary skills to teach and/or preach when called upon?

Write down your responses and share with two other persons.

5. For the next session, bring your copy of the *Book of Confessions.*

Additional Reading

2 Timothy 3:16–17
Acts 17:11; 18:28
Second Helvetic Confession, Ch. I,
BC 5.001–5.009
Westminster Confession of Faith, Ch. I,
BC 6.001–6.010
Confession of 1967, Part I, Section C.2,
BC 9.27–9.30
BO G-1.0307
BO W-2.2000

THE CHURCH AND ITS CONFESSIONS

QUESTION THREE: "Do you sincerely receive and adopt the essential tenets of the Reformed faith as expressed in the confessions of our Church as authentic and reliable expositions of what Scripture leads us to believe and do, and will you be instructed and led by those confessions as you lead the people of God?"

(BO G-14.0207c)

QUESTION FOUR: "Will you fulfill your office in obedience to Jesus Christ, under the authority of Scripture, and continually guided by our confessions?"

(BO G-14.0207d)

Our church is a confessional church. The Form of Government makes it clear how important our confessions are for us: "In these confessional statements the church declares to its members and to the world who and what it is, what it believes, what it resolves to do.

"These statements identify the Church as a community of people known by its convictions as well as by its actions" (G-2.0100).

The *Book of Confessions* is a collection of statements of faith made by the church throughout the ages. Each confession was made at a time when the church found it necessary to declare its faith. Threats from within, which might have fractured the unity of the church, or threats from without, which might have destroyed its witness, have made confessional statements necessary.

Our confessions help connect us to those who have gone before us. No single confessional statement stands alone or for all time. All are subservient to Scripture and are expressed in the language of the time in which they were written. Each confession deals with issues that were dominant at the time of writing. The Apostles' and Nicene creeds are concerned with "definitions of the mystery of the triune God and of the incarnation of the eternal Word of God in Jesus Christ" (G.2-0300). The Reformation confessions, on the other hand, are concerned about the issue of God's grace in Jesus Christ as over against a system of works righteousness which the Reformers attacked. They are also concerned about issues of the unity and peace of the church.

These confessions are more than historical documents. They are statements of the faith that continues to bind us together. "They guide the Church in its study and interpretation of the Scriptures; they summarize the essence of Christian tradition; they direct the Church in maintaining sound doctrines; they equip the Church for its work of proclamation" (G-2.0100). That is why the ordination question asks us to "receive and adopt." To receive something is to accept it and to admit its value. To adopt something is to make it one's own.

The phrase "essential tenets of the Reformed faith" is very important. We are not required to receive and adopt all that the confessions say. Various statements in the confessions are at variance with our present convictions, such as the statement in the Scots Confession that condemns "the error of the Anabaptists, who deny that children should be baptized before they have faith and understanding" (BC 3.23) or Ch. X of the Westminster Confession of Faith, which was clarified in 1903 by the Presbyterian Church in the U.S.A. in order to express "a disavowal by the Church of certain inferences drawn from statements in the Confession of Faith, and also for a declaration of certain aspects of revealed truth which appear at the present time to call for more explicit statement" (BC 6.191 and 6.193). Because the church is always being reformed by the Word of God, the confessions cannot be literally and in all details the statement of our present faith.

In spite of the differences in time, language, and issues addressed, there is a common thread that runs through the confessions. The Form of Government identifies five major Reformed themes that might be thought of as "essential tenets" (G-2.0500).

1. *"The majesty, holiness, and providence of God . . . ."* God is beyond all efforts to describe or define. God is above all that is and absolutely free to exercise both righteousness and love. No subject or concern is foreign to or alien from God.

2. *"The election of the people of God for service as well as for salvation."* God calls us into faith, and this calling is not for our own benefit only. We are faithful to God's call as we live in service to the whole world.

3. *"Covenant life marked by a disciplined concern for order in the Church according to the Word of God."* The covenant is a central symbol of the way God binds us to one another. We share in the task of keeping the church faithful in every age.

4. *"A faithful stewardship that shuns ostentation and seeks proper use of the gifts of God's creation."* Simplicity in life and worship and respect for all that God has created are basic to our understanding of our place in God's created order.

5. *"The recognition of the human tendency to idolatry and tyranny . . . ."* The corruption of sin infects both individuals and whole societies. Our obedience calls us to oppose injustice wherever it exists. From our beginning, Presbyterians have proclaimed a

message addressing people in all their relationships: family, work, nation, and world.

The confessions of the church are third in order of our commitment. They are under the supreme authority of Jesus Christ as "authentic and reliable expositions of what Scripture leads us to believe and do." The confessions are subordinate to the living Christ and to be understood as faithful interpretations of Scripture. That is why the wording of question four is so important. We fulfill the office to which we are called and elected by our "obedience to Jesus Christ," which is foremost and central. We do so "under the authority of Scripture," which is subject to the Lordship of Christ. We are "continually guided by our confessions." The degree of commitment is deliberately and consciously different for each.

JESUS CHRIST: We obey, trust, acknowledge, and believe him.

THE SCRIPTURES OF THE OLD AND NEW TESTAMENTS: We accept as witness to Jesus Christ which is unique and authoritative.

THE CONFESSIONS: We receive and adopt as "essential tenets" and are instructed and guided by them.

THE BOOK OF ORDER: We are governed by and abide by its discipline.

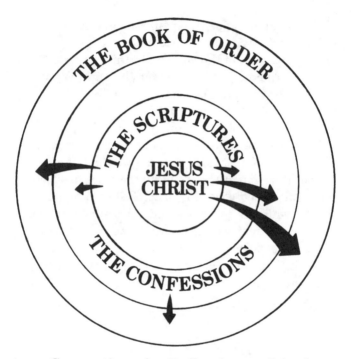

Suggestions for Reflection and Action

1. Participants individually scan the entire *Book of Confessions* to get a simple overview of the contents.

Note that some sections are short, others relatively long; some are statements of faith, others are catechism, and so on. Select one of the confessions and read carefully as much of it as you can in ten minutes.

Share your feelings, discoveries, questions with two others.

2. A family in your new-member class is considering transferring from the other Presbyterian church in town. Their dissatisfaction concerns the recent calling of a woman to be the new associate pastor. They believe firmly that the Scots Confession, which condemns women preaching the Word and administering the Sacraments, is the most reliable confession.

How would you counsel this family? How does your affirmative response to ordination questions three and four inform your response?

Work in triads (threes), and then share with the rest of the class.

3. Select one of the five major Reformed themes identified by the Form of Government as common threads running through all the confessions (see page 34 of the commentary). Find that theme in at least three of the confessions.

Work in triads, and then share with the rest of the class.

4. You are a member of the committee to draft a new confession for the year 2000. As all our confessions in the past dealt with particular situations, issues, and challenges dominant at the time of writing,

identify three contemporary issues that the Confession of 2000 might address.

Work in pairs, and then share your results with the rest of the class.

5. In the preceding question, you identified three contemporary issues that the Confession of 2000 might address. Select one of the issues and write a one- or two-sentence "confessional" paragraph that addresses the issue and which reflects obedience to the living Christ and subjection to the authority of Scripture.

Work in pairs, and then share with one other couple.

6. For the next session, bring your copy of the *Book of Order*.

Additional Reading

BO G-2.0000

THE GOVERNING OF THE CHURCH

QUESTION FIVE: "Will you be governed by our Church's polity, and will you abide by its discipline? Will you be a friend among your colleagues in ministry, working with them, subject to the ordering of God's Word and Spirit?" (BO G-14.0207e)

Important as our form of church government is, it is not essential for Christian life and witness. The Confession of 1967 affirms: "The institutions of the people of God change and vary as their mission requires in different times and places. The unity of the church is compatible with a wide variety of forms ... " (BC 9.34).

Without demeaning the value of other traditions, we believe that we are called to work together according to a particular pattern which is expressed in our *Book of Order*. Our very name, "Presbyterian," points to our high regard for church government. It is an orderly way for doing what must be done, and we do not believe that rules of procedure are at variance with our freedom in Christ. Without rules, each person resorts to what seems best or all are swayed by the strength of a powerful individual.

Our Presbyterian form of church government is rooted in our belief that the will of God is most likely to be discovered in free debate by a group of people sharing common commitment, open to the movement of the Holy Spirit, able to speak truth and to listen to others who differ, and reaching decisions only after careful hearing of all opinions and prayerful submission to God. The governing bodies of the church—session, presbytery, synod, and the General Assembly—all share in the government of the whole church. Each is given particular duties by our Constitution. Each is responsible to the next higher or more inclusive body.

Church officers are representatives of the people and are elected by them. Representation does not mean that officers are to reflect the will of the majority, but that they are to seek the will of God. We do not take polls to determine common opinion from those we represent. In our governing bodies we seek to be faithful to the trust placed in us as officers of Christ's church.

We participate in our church government as those who have promised to "be governed" by the polity of our church, so that when there is conflict we will respect the rules. When things go our way, no particular commitment to our polity is demanded; but when we lose a vote on an important issue it may be only our pledge to be governed by the system of church government that enables us to persist.

We are required to "abide by" the discipline of the church. The Rules of Discipline and the Form of Government both provide for resolution of conflict and the exercise of discipline. There are times in the life of the church when a difficult decision must be made about a matter over which there is deep disagreement. Our procedures enable us to avoid hasty conclusions until we have heard all sides and have sufficient evidence to make a fair and balanced decision.

When our conscience is troubled by a decision of a church governing body, our pledge to "abide by" the discipline of the church is particularly apt. We may be tempted to give up, to take the matter to the members of the congregation and attempt to win support for our side, or to resign in an act of protest. We abide by our system when we work within it, using the rules and means of appeal to obtain reconsideration. Our commitment to our polity requires that we accept decisions we do not like, that we work within to obtain change, and that we respect all decisions of governing bodies as possible work of the Holy Spirit when they have been fairly and freely made.

The question asks us to be "a friend among" our colleagues in ministry. Because the ordained officers of our church share in ministry, there is no place for the lone individual who claims to have all the answers directly from God. We are required to respect the decisions of others.

Elders and deacons are also colleagues with the pastor. The pastor is not responsible alone for the congregation, and when things go wrong is not the only one at fault. Because our ministry is shared, we hold ourselves and one another mutually accountable. We are called upon to take the personal risks of being honest with one another. We are also required to be patient with the behavior of another before we make a judgment. We must often work with people who remain hard to understand. Such people test our willingness to "be a friend." The New Testament defines friendship as "love," the active seeking after the good of the other person.

All our work requires that we also be "subject to the ordering of God's Word and Spirit." Our ministry is service to the One who calls us. The Word of God incarnate in Jesus Christ and witnessed to by the Scriptures is the basis for all our decisions. There are, however, issues about which Scripture is silent or unclear. We cannot expect biblical authors to have anticipated issues raised by modern technology. What we can expect is that the guidance they provide for issues of their own time will enable us to distinguish the direction of God's Spirit for us today.

The most careful attention to polity is not enough. We have a duty to be good stewards of the faith that has been given to us. That is why the Constitution requires that all meetings of church governing bodies must be opened with prayer. We submit the work before us to the leading of God's Spirit, seeking direction and correction, asking God's help for our tendency to hold on to our own opinions and prejudices.

Suggestions for Reflection and Action

1. Discuss the meaning of the word "polity." Next discuss the meaning of the word "presbyterian." Can you identify another denomination whose name suggests a particular form of government?

This exercise can be done in one open discussion.

2. Read section G-4.0301, "Presbyterian Polity," in your *Book of Order*. What are the similarities and differences between the Principles of Presbyterian Government and the United States Constitution?

Work in pairs, and then share with the rest of the class.

3. Read the Preamble to the Rules of Discipline in your *Book of Order*. Discuss the meaning of the word "discipline."

Work in threes, and then share with the rest of the class.

4. The General Assembly of the Presbyterian Church (U.S.A.) has approved a policy statement on abortion. (See Minutes of the 204th General Assembly, Part I (1992), report of the Special Committee on Problem Pregnancies and Abortion, pp. 357–377.) Governed by our church's polity and abiding by its discipline, how do you counsel those who disagree with the General Assembly's stand? How do you counsel those who agree with the decision?

Work in threes, and then share with the rest of the class.

5. Write a prayer for the opening of a session or deacons' meeting that petitions the leading of God's Spirit.

6. For the next session, bring your Bible.

Additional Reading

BO G-1.0000, 3.0000, 4.0300, 6.0100, 9.0000
Confession of 1967, Part II, Section A2,
BC 9.34–9.40
Westminster Confession of Faith, Ch. XXX/XXXII,
BC 6.196–6.172

OUR PERSONAL COMMITMENT

QUESTION SIX: "Will you in your own life seek to follow the Lord Jesus Christ, love your neighbors, and work for the reconciliation of the world?" (BO G-14.0207f)

QUESTION EIGHT: "Will you seek to serve the people with energy, intelligence, imagination, and love?" (BO G-14.0207h)

As we answer question six, we commit ourselves to following our words by our actions. The promise to follow Jesus Christ as Lord is an acknowledgment that we who lead have a duty to model the Christian life. We are watched more closely than others in the church. The Form of Government says of the ordained, ". . . those who undertake particular ministries should be persons of strong faith, dedicated discipleship, and love of Jesus Christ as Savior and Lord. Their manner of life should be a demonstration of the Christian gospel in the Church and in the world" (G.0106).

We would all rather escape the responsibility of being models for others. Our hesitations and fears do not, however, alter the situation. If an elder is engaged in dishonest business practices, that person brings rebuke upon the whole church. Those who are set apart by ordination are given great responsibility.

We need to ask ourselves, What must we do because we are Christians and what must we cease doing because of our faith? Our answers to these questions are not easily discovered, nor is the task of ordering our lives to express our answer painless.

The ordination question provides only a two-part guide for our behavior. We are asked to love our neighbors and to "work for the reconciliation of the world." Love of neighbors is central to the demand of Jesus. It requires that we seek the good for all those who cross our path. Jesus' definition of neighbor includes people we never see, who live in faraway places and are different from us.

Love of neighbor is closely related to reconciliation of the world. Both include all that we do, the way we earn and spend our money, the way we treat the world's resources, and the way we vote. A great deal is expected of us, and the demand is too much to bear alone. We need the nurture of the whole church, both of other officers and of members. We need their prayers and encouragement. We also need to be renewed for our tasks by the development of our own devotional life. In prayer, we are renewed for our work, strengthened for burdens, and enabled to widen our horizons by fellowship with Jesus Christ.

Question eight adds to the responsibility placed upon us by calling on us to give our very best to the work to which we have been called. Although each of us has certain natural gifts, we are expected to develop new gifts by self-discipline.

Energy comes from within, from the power of enthusiastic commitment. Energy can be drained from us as we grow weary and allow ourselves to be so busy doing good that we forget to care for ourselves. To serve with energy is to seek renewal through prayer, relaxation, rest, and occasions for laughter and play.

We serve with intelligence when we study the issues before us and become well informed about matters requiring our attention. When we act on the basis of uninformed opinion, great harm can be done to the church of Jesus Christ. Although we cannot have all the answers, we are responsible to read, study, and engage in conversation with those who know more or have more personal experience with particular issues than we. Every church officer is to be a good interpreter of the worldwide work of our denomination. We need to be able to respond to criticisms, not out of defensiveness, but with information that comes from reliable sources. To join with those who criticize, having only read the critics, is irresponsible and unintelligent. Thought and judgment are essential qualities for our work.

Imagination is dreaming dreams that go beyond what we do. To be imaginative is to allow ourselves to be stirred by new ideas and willing to give them a hearing. The gift of imagination is easily destroyed by dull conformity to accustomed patterns. To keep the gift of imagination alive requires that we stay open to new possibilities and have the courage to dare to try that which is risky. The new is always dangerous, but the way of a new life in Christ is just such an adventure.

To serve with love is to remember other people at all times and to keep their needs uppermost in our minds as we make our decisions. The cost of loving others may be that we are criticized as being soft or even obstinate. Yet the terrible cruelty that may take place even in the church is a contradiction of all that Christ calls us to be as his body. Whenever persons are made subordinate to "what is good for the church," we are guilty of acting without love. We are required to take love seriously as the instrument of our decisions and the shape of policies. It is better to make the wrong decision out of love than to arrive at a well designed and carefully worked out policy without love.

Both question six and question eight are person-
ally demanding. They call upon us to exercise our
commitment to be responsible leaders. Our own resources are never enough for this high calling and
awesome responsibility. We can only seek to follow
as Christ empowers and as we are nurtured by others and by our own prayers, and are fed by the fellowship of worship.

Suggestions for Reflection and Action

1. Reread the first three paragraphs. Use the following reader reaction method: Put (!) at those
points that stimulate a new idea or bring a new insight; (X) at those points at which you disagree with
the writer; and (?) at those points that are unclear
or which you would like to discuss.

Compare your responses with the rest of the class
in open discussion.

2. What are some ways in which you can set a personal example as well as lead your congregation to-
ward love of neighbors and working for the
reconciliation of the world?

Work in threes, and then share with the rest of
the class.

3. Working in pairs, share with each other the
gifts you bring to your position of leadership. Re-
turning to one large group, introduce your partner

to the rest of the class by calling attention to his/ her gifts.

4. Working in threes, discuss the following questions: What are some barriers to your fulfilling the mandate in ordination question eight? What will help to encourage you? What vision do you bring to the church? Share your responses with the rest of the class.

5. Read *Mark 2:23–3:6*. How does this passage inform your commitment to serve the church?
Work individually, and then share with two other people.

6. Rank from easiest (1) to most difficult (4) the following qualifications for leadership:

_____ energy

_____ intelligence

_____ imagination

_____ love

Discuss your rankings with one other person.

7. For the next session, bring your Bible.

Additional Reading

BO G-3.0000
BO G-4.0400
BO G-5.0100
BO G-6.0200, 6.0300, 6.0400
BO W-6.0000, 7.0000

PEACE, UNITY, AND PURITY

QUESTION SEVEN: "Do you promise to further the peace, unity, and purity of the Church?" (BO G-14.0207g)

Each of us has a vision of what the church ought to be, and we see the existing church as less than Christ intended. We are, therefore, at times discouraged by the difference. It is our own faith that causes us to be critical of the pettiness, the narrowness of vision, the intolerance and bigotry, and the lack of commitment that we sometimes experience in the church.

Chapter III of the Form of Government holds before us all a very high view of the church. "The Church of Jesus Christ is the provisional demonstration of what God intends for all of humanity. The Church is called to be a sign in and for the world of the new reality which God has made available to people in Jesus Christ" (G-3.0200). We must never be satisfied with the church as it is. Our ordination/installation vow requires us to be agents by which the faithfulness and obedience to Christ which the church must exhibit are brought to actualization. That is the meaning of the purity of the church. We are to do this by ". . . healing and reconciling and binding up wounds, ministering to the needs of the poor, the sick, the lonely, and the powerless, engaging in the struggle to free people from sin, fear, oppression, hunger, and injustice" (G-3.0300). Our commitment to such high ideals often makes us very impatient with the church.

At the same time, we promise to further the peace of the church. Peace is not simply the absence of conflict. It can only come about when we face our differences openly, in the confidence that it is Jesus Christ who holds us together. Our diversity is not something to be feared, but something to be cherished. The Form of Government makes this clear: " . . . The fellowship of Christians as it gathers for worship and orders its corporate life will display a rich variety of form, practice, language, program, nurture, and service to suit culture and need" (G-4.0401). Our diversity can frighten us. We need to remember the image of the church as the body of Christ. As the eye is not the foot nor the hand the ear, but each part acts out its role and makes the whole body function properly, so we, though different, are part of a single body. Our differences are a gift. We need one another. Those with whom we disagree may help to keep us honest.

Peace cannot come about when we are afraid. When some people rule by intimidating the rest, or when everyone pretends to agree but privately feels isolated or unheard, there is seething conflict. The terrible fights that occasionally break out in the church are the result of forced peace at the price of integrity and honesty.

The unity of the church is always fragile. The body is fractured when some person or group loses sight of the need for correction by others. Unity does not mean uniformity. It means that we are to respect one another and trust that each person is seeking to be faithful to Jesus Christ, however different the position that is expressed. The Form of Government says about our visible unity: "Visible oneness, by which a diversity of persons, gifts, and understandings is brought together, is an important sign of the unity of God's people" (G-4.0203).

The peace and unity of the church are always in tension with its purity. To work only for the purity of the church can shatter its unity and break its peace. One the other hand, to settle for unity at the price of faithfulness is to adjust too quickly to a church that is less than God calls it to be.

To further the peace, unity, and purity of the

church is a struggle that is sometimes painful. We cannot always have our own way. I cannot be sure that I have the right answers. Diversity must be seen as more than a necessary or temporary evil to be corrected as soon as my group can win and either change, correct, or drive out all those who differ.

Our peace comes not from avoiding conflict but from mutual respect. Our unity comes not only from adherence to the *Book of Order,* but from Jesus Christ, whose servants we all are. Our purity does not come from narrow legalism but comes from seeking together to be faithful, in the knowledge that there is always more light to be shed from God's Word.

There are times when each of us has to decide whether or not the action of the church violates our conscience. If it does, and all appeals to process in our system fail, then we have the option of peaceful withdrawal. Withdrawal must be a very reluctant act, done only after we have exhausted every effort.

To be a Presbyterian means to trust the process by which the elected representatives of God's people, meeting together, arrive at decisions with care and thoughtfulness. We may not always agree with the results, but we respect our colleagues and trust that they have done their best to be faithful to the One who calls us together in our differences and demands that we live as one people.

Suggestions for Reflection and Action

1. Write a one-sentence response to each of the following questions: What is your vision of what the church ought to be? How does the church presently fall short of what Christ intends the church to be? As a church officer, how can you help to bring the church closer to what Christ intends the church to be?

In groups of three, share your responses. Then compare your responses with the first four paragraphs of the commentary.

2. Read *1 Cor. 12.12–26*. How does this passage guide your thought and action regarding the peace and unity of the church?

Work in groups of three, and then share with the rest of the class.

3. Your church has never ordained women to be elders. You are now required by the Constitution to change that tradition. Divide the class into three groups, and ask each group to identify as deeply as possible with one of the following perspectives: (*a*) working only for peace in the church; (*b*) working only for unity in the church; and (*c*) working only for purity in the church.

After a sufficient amount of time to prepare arguments from the assigned perspective, the three groups will come together (each group sitting

together). Using your imaginations, role-play a debate about ordaining women elders.

Close by discussing how you can preserve peace,
unity, and purity in the church.

Additional Reading

BO G-1.0200
BO G-3.0400
BO G-4.0200, .0302, .0303
BO G-4.0400
BO W-7.0000
Westminster Confession of Faith, Ch. XXX/XXXII,
BC 6.169–6.172
Confession of 1967, Part II, Section A.2,
BC 9.34–9.40
Second Helvetic Confession, Ch. XVII, BC 5.132,
5.133, 5.134, 5.135, 5.140, 5.141
Brief Statement of Faith, 10.4, BC 10.4

SESSION VIII

DUTIES
OF THE OFFICE

QUESTION NINE (for elder): "Will you be a faithful elder, watching over the people, providing for their worship, nurture, and service? Will you share in government and discipline, serving in governing bodies of the Church, and in your ministry will you try to show the love and justice of Jesus Christ?" (BO G-14.0207i)

QUESTION NINE (for deacon): "Will you be a faithful deacon, teaching charity, urging concern, and directing the people's help to the friendless and those in need? In your ministry will you try to show the love and justice of Jesus Christ?"
(BO G-14.0207j)

While the final ordination/installation question varies with the particular office, there are common threads even here. Elders, deacons, and ministers are all asked, "In your ministry, will you try to show

the love and justice of Jesus Christ?" All ordained
officers share in ministry with the people who have
elected them to leadership. It is unfortunate that
our word "minister" has come to have a double
meaning. We get confused as to whether we are
speaking of the ministry of the whole people of God
or of the particular ministry of those ordained to the
ministry of the Word and Sacrament. In ordination
we share a common ministry, even though our particular duties are not the same.

Elders and ministers of the Word and Sacrament
both take the vow to take part in "government and
discipline, serving in (the) governing bodies of the
church." Being active in presbytery is not a luxury
for those who are so inclined but a basic element in
the ministry of both elders and ministers. It is unfortunate that we tend to view service in presbytery,
synod, and General Assembly as taking away from
the work of the congregation or as getting in the
way of the congregation's witness and ministry.

Our connectional system depends upon the ordained officers to be the glue that holds things together. Our affirmative answer to this ordination
question commits us to the work of the larger
church so that we can all help to interpret and support that work. Only when all parts of the church
are represented and fully participating does our system of church government work properly. Elders

who participate in the life of presbytery prevent that body from becoming a club for ministers. They represent a perspective on the church that only comes from those whose work is in the world and who are not dependent upon the institutional church for their livelihood. The balance between ministers and elders in every governing body above the session is very important, and our ordination is a sign of our commitment to this full participation.

The duties of elders are spelled out in some detail in the Form of Government (G-6.0301-.0304). Elders share with the ministers of the Word and Sacrament in the government of the church, which includes the responsibility for decision-making regarding nearly every part of the life of the church. The session is responsible for the worship, education, budget, evangelism, and organizational structures of the congregation. But the session is more than a structure for power and decisions. It is the responsibility of elders to care for the people of the congregation, to visit them, pray with them, and inform the pastor when there is particular need. This personal ministry of elders is as important as their governmental function, and must be kept in balance with it or decisions may be arrived at with too little attention to the people who are affected by them.

The duties of deacons are also listed in the Form of Government. In the form of the ordination/

installation questions for deacons, the duties are made clear, "teaching charity, urging concern, and directing the people's help to the friendless and those in need." Although the office of deacon is not mandatory, it is one that complements that of the elder. Deacons have a special responsibility to serve as the conscience of the congregation, both in their own service and in bringing before session situations of particular need that they discover. The Form of Government indicates that the duty of the deacon is, " . . . first of all, to minister to those who are in need, to the sick, to the friendless, and to any who may be in distress" (G-6.0402). Although deacons work under the direction of the session, their work is not less important. In a hurting world, deacons represent the passionate concern of Christ for those who are hurting, wherever they may be. That breadth of concern leads deacons to go beyond the immediate area of the congregation, reaching out and assisting the whole church to heal the hurts of people around the world.

Our world requires the full ministry of the church. One pastor alone cannot be the sole minister. The commitment and service of all elders and deacons is necessary if the church is to be responsible and really available for the many different needs of every community. The strength of our Presbyterian system is the motivation and engagement of those who share in ministry with the pastors.

Election to church office is not simply an honor to be enjoyed. Ministry means service, and we are all set apart to be servants to Jesus Christ through the service we render in and through the church. In our collective service, we enable the congregation to move beyond survival issues to faithfulness to Christ in our local communities and around the world. This service is badly needed in a frightened and confused world. We are all called upon to take risks that offer hope for the fears we all share, and to be faithful to our Lord in a world where compromise and falsehood are often taken for granted.

Suggestions for Reflection and Action

1. In pairs (one deacon and one elder), share how you feel about being called to common ministry with the pastor(s).

2. You have agreed to show the love and justice of Jesus Christ in your ministry. Can you have one without the other? What is the danger of sharing love without justice? justice without love?

Discuss in triads, and then share with the larger group.

3. Role-play the following situation: The pastor has, on several occasions, expressed the feeling that presbytery is a "waste of time." How would you, as an elder, give counsel in light of your understanding of our connectional system?

4. ELDERS: Read the Form of Government (G-6.0300), paying careful attention to the section on specific responsibilities. Then rank in order those responsibilities of greatest interest and concern to you.

Share your ranking with one other person.

5. DEACONS: Read Form of Government (G-6.0400), paying careful attention to the section on specific responsibilities. From what you know about your congregation and the larger community, identify three needs or hurts that you would want your congregation to address.

Work individually, and then share with two other people.

Additional Reading

BO G-4.0300–4.0400
BO G-6.0100
1 Timothy 3:1–13
Titus 1:5–9